The Life of
CORGNELIUS
and
STUMPHREY

The Cutest Corgis in the World

SUSIE BROOKS

The Life of Corgnelius and Stumphrey

ISBN-13: 978-0-373-89314-0

Library of Congress Catalog-in-publication data on file with the publisher.

www.Harlequin.com

Printed in U.S.A.

DEDICATED TO:

Justin: You're one of the most wonderful people I've ever met in my life, thank you for being such a great best friend.

Big Sis: I'd say something like, "Thank you for always being there for me," but that's not our style. So I'll just say, "Don't you look at that BIRD!!"

My Rolling Family (excluding Ravi): I love you. Here's to a lifetime of bright lights and long nights.

Hey, there! This is Corgnelius. He's a corgi.

He doesn't want to brag or anything but... He's got a pretty great life. Just take a look for yourself!

He starts off each day with breakfast in bed.

Then hops
online to check
his facebook page
and answer any
fan mail.

(This would be so much easier
if he knew how to type.)

Next, he takes a quick shower. (This isn't the highlight of his day, but he powers through it.)

Whew, it's finally over!

He then peruses his
wardrobe and decides
what to wear.

Maybe something casual?

Or if he's got an important meeting, he'll put on the ol' monkey suit. (Ah, the burdens of the corporate world.)

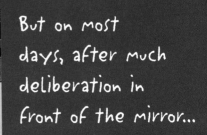

But on most days, after much deliberation in front of the mirror...

He usually goes with no clothes at all, because nothing complements fur better than fur.

Next, he needs to figure out how to wear his ears. Maybe down?

To the side?

Just let them fall
naturally? Yup, that's
the one!

Oh my goodness, look at the time. Corgnelius is going to be late for work!

The dog park is not going to manage itself!

What does he do as a manager? More like what doesn't he do? And the answer is nothing, because he does everything.

As a manager, he makes sure every dog gets at least one hug

He also oversees any and all construction digs.

He monitors tail length and makes sure no one's tail is too long. (In his opinion, anything longer than a bunny nub is excessive, but to each his own.)

He also gets called in to investigate potentially hazardous materials.

And remove them from the premises, if need be. Nothing to see here, people, just a handsome hero doing his job!

Even though it's a dog park, he chats with the humans and makes sure they're having a good time. (I mean, two legs, no fur...it's the least he can do for these poor things.)

He even lets them pet him.
(It makes them so happy.)

But he still has to keep an eye on them...
they tend to steal the toys.

Corgnelius is also the park's peacekeeper, stepping in to break up fights.

On top of all of this, he manages to supervise the water bowl and makes sure no one sneezes in it.

Every once in a while, another
corgi comes along and tries to
usurp Corgnelius's position. As the
law of the land goes, if another
corgi can keep him on his back
for at least thirty seconds,
he becomes the new leader.

Oh no...

It's already been twenty seconds!

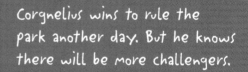

Corgnelius wins to rule the park another day. But he knows there will be more challengers.

He has to watch his back.

After a long, exhausting day, Corgnelius heads home.

He can't wait to climb into his favorite chair and relax.

Climb...into...his...favorite...

Actually, the floor is good. The floor is much better than the chair. It's perfect.

Then he usually
partakes in
a snack.

Or two.

Or three... Hey! Don't judge him!
He has a very stressful job, okay?!

After he finishes his one or three snacks, it's time for dinner. **Ahem,** dinner, he said.

Excuse me...
dinner....

Finally! Geez.

Then of course, some after-dinner drinks.

What? Did you say dessert? Nooo... I couldn't...

Well...if you insist!

Before he knows it, it's already time for bed.

Thank goodness he has the next day off.

On these rare days off,
Corgnelius loves to work on his tan.

He makes sure to rotate his head to get some color on those front stumps.

But...

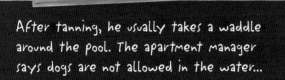

After tanning, he usually takes a waddle around the pool. The apartment manager says dogs are not allowed in the water...

Sometimes he
just can't resist.

3½ FT

You never saw him here, got it?!

After all that physical exertion, he likes to work out his mind, too.

He recommends this book;
all the characters are
ridiculously good-looking.

After such a physically and mentally demanding day, Corgnelius just likes to kick his feet back and relax for the night.

Yep, life is pretty perfect. But little does Corgnelius know that life is never going to be the same again...

A gigantic...

Yet tiny...

Change...

Named Stumphrey.

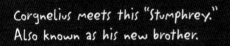
Corgnelius meets this "Stumphrey."
Also known as his new brother.

Corgnelius inspects him.

Thoroughly.

He comes to the conclusion that he doesn't need Stumphrey around. Thanks, but no thanks.

Then we break it to him that Stumphrey's here to stay. And that they're going to be brothers forever.

And it's been replaced
with this life.

This new life of getting food stolen.

And toys taken.

Even when he does have something to himself, he's constantly being watched.

It's called privacy,
Stumphrey! GEEZ!

Did Corgnelius also mention the completely unprovoked attacks?

(Although, we have mentioned to Corgnelius that using Stumphrey as a soccer ball might be considered provocation.)

Same with refusing to share toys that he clearly doesn't need anymore.

But he does use his teething toy! He uses it all the time!

And when Corgnelius tries to tell Stumphrey not to touch his things, all he gets back is attitude.

And more attitude. Ugh, he can't take this anymore!

So Corgnelius goes to a therapist and tells him all
about Stumphrey and what a nightmare he is.

At home, he reflects on what the therapist said: "Life changes and you have to be strong and stumpy enough to adapt to these changes. Instead of focusing on all the negative things about Stumphrey, think about all the positive things."

Well...maybe it is helpful to have someone around to tell him when he's got something on his face.

And...it is much better to have someone to watch scary movies with.

And when Stumphrey needs help...

Corgnelius does enjoy being the hero.

Corgnelius does have to admit, Stumphrey looks pretty handsome in his hand-me-downs.

It's nice to have someone around to talk to.

And laugh with.

Corgnelius feels honored when he's trusted with a secret. He's never been told a secret before.

Because this carrot sure doesn't tell him anything.

It's also pretty cool that he has an instant pillow whenever he needs one.

Now he has someone to go to fourth of July BBQs with.

And to celebrate Christmas with.

And Halloween.

And the most important holiday of all—his birthday.
It's May 18, in case you were wondering... And the ratio
of dog to human years is 7:1, so if you wanted to give
him seven presents, he wouldn't be mad or anything.

Stumphrey also makes a good copilot on long car rides.

And doesn't judge him for his awesome taste in vacation attire.

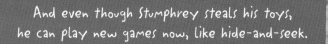

And even though Stumphrey steals his toys,
he can play new games now, like hide-and-seek.

It's especially fun with a partner who's not good at it.

Tug-of-war with the human is also a lot more effective with a partner.

Because honestly, it was just a losing battle when he was by himself.

They also have some pretty epic tickle fights.

Who knew having a dining buddy
could be so much fun?

And it's weird, but food actually tastes better when someone else wants it.

Now that Stumphrey's around, he finally has a beach bud.

A companion to explore
the shores with.

And Stumphrey's not afraid to get his nose dirty when they want to search for buried treasure.

Those boring black-tie work functions won't be so bad with a plus one.

And Stumphrey definitely makes going to the vet a lot less scary. I mean...tedious... He meant tedious. He's not scared...of those sharp needles... Don't be ridiculous.

And Corgnelius can finally pass down all his wisdom. Like how to properly destroy a shoe.

Or package.

Or chair. He doesn't want to brag or anything, but he's very knowledgeable in the art of destruction.

And whenever he lands himself in jail,
Stumphrey's around to try to break hi[m]

Or, better yet,
serve time with him.

As Corgnelius's therapist said, even though Stumphrey's a part of his life now, he doesn't have to be with him twenty-four hours a day.

They can still do their own things.

And have separate schedules.

They can totally be their own dog.

With separate interests.

It's not like they're joined at the hip or anything...

Yup, Corgnelius's life was pretty perfect.

But it's even more perfect now that Stumphrey's in it.

I'd like to thank the following people:

CORGNELIUS and STUMPHREY'S friends on FACEBOOK, INSTAGRAM and TUMBLR. I definitely feel the love you guys have for these two with every "like" and comment you leave. This book is for you. I hope you enjoy it!

REBECCA HUNT, my wonderful editor, and Harlequin, my publishing company, for reaching out to me and making this book happen. Because of you, I'll be able to nonchalantly introduce myself as an internationally published author, and I will forever be grateful for that bragging right.

DANIEL GALLEY for tolerating my incessant corgi-filled conversations five days a week. Thanks for all the love and support!

MATT STOPERA and the rest of the staff at BUZZFEED, thank you for every corgi-related article you put out. Your efforts to educate the world on how awesome these dogs are should truly be commended.

THE FROGMAN (http://thefrogman.me/) and CORGI ADDICT (http://corgiaddict.com/), for reblogging Corgnelius's photos when I was just starting his blog. I attribute the gain of his first 100, then first 1,000 followers, to these two websites and I thank you both.

DEANNA and PUDGE, (http://pudge.corgiaddict.com/) stumbling upon your blog and looking at all of Pudge's pictures was the reason I became obsessed with corgis and knew I needed some of my own one day. Thank you for sharing Pudge with the world.

About the Author

Susie Brooks lives in Los Angeles with her husband Justin and, of course, their two boys, Corgnelius and Stumphrey. She spends most of her time at home doing ordinary things like taking four hundred photos a day of her dogs, hugging them, sniffing their corn chip paws, crying and wondering why they're so perfect, watching them sleep, etc. In her spare time she enjoys going to concerts and music festivals with her friends.